UNDER THE HOOD

THE HISTORY OF
LAMBORGHINIS

SETH KINGSTON

PowerKiDS
press.

NEW YORK

Published in 2019 by The Rosen Publishing Group, Inc.
29 East 21st Street, New York, NY 10010

Copyright 2013; revised edition 2019

Editor: Elizabeth Krajnik
Book Design: Michael Flynn

Photo Credits: Cover (car) VanderWolf Images/Shutterstock.com; cover, p. 1 (emblem) Roberto Lusso/Shutterstock.com; cover, pp. 1, 3, 6–14, 16–20, 22–24, 26, 28–32 (background) fotomak/Shutterstock.com; p. 5 (Ferruccio Lamborghini) Jean-Claude Deutsch/Paris Match Archive/Getty Images; p. 5 (emblem) meunierd/Shutterstock.com; p. 6 Mondadori Portfolio/Mondadori Portfolio Premium/Getty Images; p. 7 United Archives GmbH/Alamy Stock Photo; p. 9 (Countach) Martyn Lucy/Getty Images Sport/Getty Images; pp. 9 (350 GT), 19 (motor) Sergey Kohl/Shutterstock.com; p. 11 (racecar) https://commons.wikimedia.org/wiki/File:Aguri_Suzuki_demonstrating_Lola_LC90_2012_Japan.jpg; p. 11 (Aguri Suzuki) Pascal Rondeau/Getty Images Sport/Getty Images; p. 13 John Crouch/Icon Sportswire/Getty Images; p. 15 Auto BILD Syndication/ullstein bild/Getty Images; p. 16 Clari Massimiliano/Shutterstock.com; p. 17 Andrew Burton/Getty Images News/Getty Images; p. 19 (inset) dimcars/Shutterstock.com; p. 21 yousang/Shutterstock.com; p. 23 (orange Lamborghini) Jason Harper/Bloomberg/Getty Images; p. 23 (red Lamborghini) https://commons.wikimedia.org/wiki/File:Lamborghini_Gallardo_LP570-4_Spyder_Performante_-_Ben_in_london_2.jpg; p. 24 Pan Xunbin/Shutterstock.com; p. 25 Marukosu/Shutterstock.com; p. 27 (Urus) testing/Shutterstock.com; p. 27 (Veneno Roadster) Dong liu/Shutterstock.com; pp. 28–29 Chesnot/Getty Images News/Getty Images.

Library of Congress Cataloging-in-Publication Data

Names: Kingston, Seth, author.
Title: The history of Lamborghinis / Seth Kingston.
Description: New York : PowerKids Press, [2019] | Series: Under the hood | Includes index.
Identifiers: LCCN 2018030329| ISBN 9781538343395 (library bound) | ISBN 9781538344545 (pbk.) | ISBN 9781538344552 (6 pack)
Subjects: LCSH: Lamborghini automobile–History–Juvenile literature.
Classification: LCC TL215.L33 K56 2019 | DDC 629.222–dc23
LC record available at https://lccn.loc.gov/2018030329

Manufactured in the United States of America

CPSIA Compliance Information: Batch #CWPK19. For Further Information contact Rosen Publishing, New York, New York at 1-800-237-9932

||| CONTENTS |||

THE BIRTH OF THE
CHARGING BULL

On April 28, 1916, Ferruccio Lamborghini, the founder of Automobili Lamborghini, was born in Cento, Italy. Lamborghini grew up in a grape-farming family and trained to become a **mechanic**. His training helped him during World War II, when he was a mechanic in the Italian armed forces. As a young man, he was interested in fast cars and made changes to them to make them go faster.

From these humble beginnings was born a man who would create some of the most sought-after sports cars in history. Today, most Lamborghinis have 12-**cylinder** engines. Powerful engines and **innovation** keep Lamborghinis on the cutting edge of supercars. Many people are able to quickly recognize a Lamborghini because the cars look **futuristic**, sleek, and stylish.

START YOUR ENGINES

MOST TYPES OF LAMBORGHINIS ARE NAMED AFTER FAMOUS BULLS AND BULL BREEDS. FOR EXAMPLE, THE LAMBORGHINI MIURA IS NAMED AFTER A BREED OF BULLS BRED BY DON FERNANDO MIURA FERNANDEZ, WHOSE RANCH FERRUCCIO LAMBORGHINI HAD VISITED.

THE LAMBORGHINI LOGO

The first Lamborghini logo was a bull on a red shield with a black outline. Today, the Lamborghini logo is a golden charging bull on a black background. Paolo Rambaldi created the Lamborghini logo. He chose the bull because it's the **symbol** for the **astrological** sign Taurus, which is Ferruccio Lamborghini's astrological sign. The bull is also a symbol of aggressiveness, or readiness to fight. The logo also refers to Lamborghini's competition with Ferrari, whose logo is a **prancing** black horse.

FERRUCCIO LAMBORGHINI DIED ON FEBRUARY 20, 1993, IN PERUGIA, ITALY. HE WAS 76 YEARS OLD.

STARTING WITH
TRACTORS

After World War II, Lamborghini founded a tractor manufacturing business. His first tractors were built using spare parts from German tanks. Before making sports cars, Lamborghini also produced heating systems and air conditioners, making him a very wealthy man. In late 1962, Lamborghini began working on a sports car that could compete with Ferrari and other sports car manufacturers.

START YOUR ENGINES

A V-12 ENGINE IS AN ENGINE THAT HAS 12 CYLINDERS ARRANGED IN A "V" SHAPE. THE MORE CYLINDERS AN ENGINE HAS, THE MORE POWERFUL IT IS.

WHEN FERRUCCIO LAMBORGHINI RETIRED, HE DECIDED TO PLANT GRAPES TO MAKE WINE. ONE OF LAMBORGHINI'S MOST FAMOUS WINES IS NAMED COLLI DI TRASIMENO OR, MORE COMMONLY, SANGUE DI MIURA, WHICH MEANS "MIURA BLOOD" IN ITALIAN.

In May 1963, Lamborghini founded Automobili Ferruccio Lamborghini and built a state-of-the-art factory in Sant'Agata Bolognese, Italy. Lamborghini's first car, the Lamborghini 350 GTV, a **prototype**, made its debut, or first appearance, at the Turin Auto Show in November 1963. It was a coupe, or hardtop with two seats and two doors, with a V-12 engine. In 1971, Ferruccio Lamborghini decided to retire. He later sold his company. Volkswagen currently owns Lamborghini.

THE LAMBORGHINI LOOK

Since the first Lamborghini came out in 1963, the way Lamborghinis look has changed a great deal. The first Lamborghinis looked similar to other sports cars, such as Ferraris. Ferruccio Lamborghini's goal was to produce cars that made people standing on the sides of the road turn their heads.

The prototype of the Lamborghini Countach was introduced at the 1971 Geneva Car Show. It introduced the world to the now-**signature** wedge shape of Lamborghinis. Wedge-shaped cars have a wide but short front, and they get taller in the back. The Countach was also the first Lamborghini to have scissor doors, which lift up instead of pulling out when opened. Lamborghini has continued to produce cars that challenge common car **designs** while staying true to its signature look.

LAMBORGHINIS MOVED AWAY FROM THE SOFT LINES OF THE FIRST CARS AND NOW HAVE AN EASILY RECOGNIZED DESIGN THAT'S BECOME A KNOWN SYMBOL OF WEALTH AND SUCCESS.

1965 LAMBORGHINI 350 GT

LAMBORGHINI COUNTACH

9

MAKING ENGINES FOR
FORMULA ONE

Formula One is a type of racing in which drivers race single-seat racecars on a combination of city streets and racetracks around the world. These races are called grands prix. Formula One racecars are the fastest in the world, reaching up to 220 miles (354.1 km) per hour. Even though Lamborghini makes very fast cars, it's never formed a Formula One racing team.

In late 1987, French Formula One team Larrousse asked designer Mauro Forghieri to create a new engine for them. Forghieri asked Lamborghini to work with him on the project. The LE3512, a 3.5-liter, V-12 engine, at times powered cars for the Larrousse, Lotus, Ligier, Minardi, and Modena racing teams. In 1992, the Chrysler company, which then owned Lamborghini, reduced its production numbers. Lamborghini could no longer afford to take part in Formula One.

LARROUSSE DRIVER AGURI SUZUKI TOOK THIRD PLACE AT THE 1990 JAPANESE GRAND PRIX DRIVING A LOLA LC90, WHICH HAD THE LE3512 ENGINE. THIS IS THE BEST A LAMBORGHINI ENGINE DID IN A FORMULA ONE RACE.

AGURI SUZUKI

LAMBORGHINIS IN
RACING

Squadra Corse is Lamborghini's racing division. It includes the Lamborghini Super Trofeo series, GT Customer Racing, and Lamborghini Accademia. Super Trofeo is Lamborghini's one-make series, which means only one type of car takes part in the races. As of 2018, drivers in each of the three continental series—Europe, Asia, and North America—race the Huracán Super Trofeo Evo. Super Trofeo is the fastest one-make series in the world. Lamborghini Super Trofeo Europe celebrated its 10th **edition** in 2018.

Lamborghini GT Customer Racing is a series in which Automobili Lamborghini competes against other constructors in Gran Turismo races. GT racing is a type of **endurance** racing. As of 2018, drivers in GT Customer Racing use the Huracán GT3 as their racing car. GT cars look very similar to production cars but are much more powerful.

LAMBORGHINI ACCADEMIA

Lamborghini Accademia is Squadra Corse's driving school, in which students can learn how to drive a Lamborghini. Track Accademia allows students to learn to drive a Lamborghini like a racecar and Winter Accademia gives them the chance to learn to drive a Lamborghini on ice and snow. Pilota Lamborghini is a coaching program that helps just four participants at a time become better drivers who are ready for real racing at the Las Vegas Motor Speedway.

GT RACES TAKE PLACE AROUND THE WORLD. THE IMSA WEATHERTECH SPORTSCAR CHAMPIONSHIP IS THE UNITED STATES' GT CHAMPIONSHIP RACE.

START YOUR ENGINES

THE AMERICAN LE MANS SERIES (ALMS) WAS A TYPE OF GT RACING THAT CONSISTED OF ENDURANCE AND SPRINT RACES. ALMS RACES TOOK PLACE IN THE UNITED STATES AND CANADA. IN 2013, ALMS JOINED THE GRAND-AM SPORTS CAR SERIES TO BECOME UNITED SPORTSCAR RACING.

THE 350 GT
1964–1966

Ferruccio Lamborghini's first car was the 350 GT. GT stands for "grand tourer." A grand tourer is a car that's designed to be comfortable to drive for long distances. The 350 GT is a two-door coupe. From 1964 to 1966, Carrozzeria Touring, an Italian car-building company, made 120 of these cars for Lamborghini.

The 350 GT was the production model of the 350 GTV prototype. From the 350 GT, Carrozzeria Touring made two spyder, or convertible, **versions**, which were both called the 350 GTS. Another model based on the 350 GT was the 400 GT, which had a four-liter engine. There were 273 of these cars made.

Lamborghini made the 350 GT to compete with Ferraris. He wanted his new car to be faster, better looking, and more powerful than any of Ferrari's cars.

THE 350 GT HAD 280 HORSEPOWER AND COULD GO UP TO 160 MILES (257.5 KM) PER HOUR. IT COULD REACH 62 MILES (100 KM) PER HOUR IN 6.8 SECONDS AND REACH 100 MILES (160.9 KM) PER HOUR IN 16.3 SECONDS.

THE COUNTACH
1974–1990

The Countach was made from 1974 until 1990, and 2,000 of the cars were sold. Lamborghini made five different production models of the Countach: the LP400, the LP400 S, the LP500 S, the LP5000 Quattrovalvole, and the 25th Anniversary.

The first generation of the Countach was the Countach LP400. LP stands for *longitudinale posteriore*, which means "longitudinal back" in Italian. It refers to the rear engine, which was mounted lengthwise. The Countach LP400 was produced from 1974 until 1978, and 151 cars were made.

25TH ANNIVERSARY

THE COUNTACH LP400 S SERIES III, PICTURED HERE, HAD A V-12 ENGINE THAT PRODUCED 375 HORSEPOWER. THE CAR HAD A TOP SPEED OF 179.8 MILES (289.4 KM) PER HOUR.

The Countach was a two-seater that was very low to the ground. The Countach's engine was in the back of the car rather than in the front. Because of this, the driver and passenger seats were pushed forward.

THE DIABLO
1990–2001

The Diablo was made to replace the Countach. When the Diablo was introduced in 1990, it was the fastest production car ever made, with a top speed of 202 miles (325.1 km) per hour. It could go from 0 to 62 miles (0 to 100 km) per hour in 4.5 seconds and get to 80 miles (128.7 km) per hour in 9.6 seconds. The first Diablo had a 5.7-liter V-12 engine that produced 492 horsepower. This model had two-wheel drive, but a model with four-wheel drive soon followed.

The 2001 Diablo VT 6.0 and VT 6.0 SE were the last Diablos produced. The VT 6.0 was more powerful than the first generation of Diablos. It had 550 horsepower and could reach 60 miles (96.6 km) per hour in 3.4 seconds.

THE DIABLO WAS WIDE, SAT LOW TO THE GROUND, AND LOOKED FUTURISTIC. MANY CAR LOVERS AROUND THE WORLD LIKED THE DIABLO. ALMOST 3,000 DIABLOS WERE SOLD.

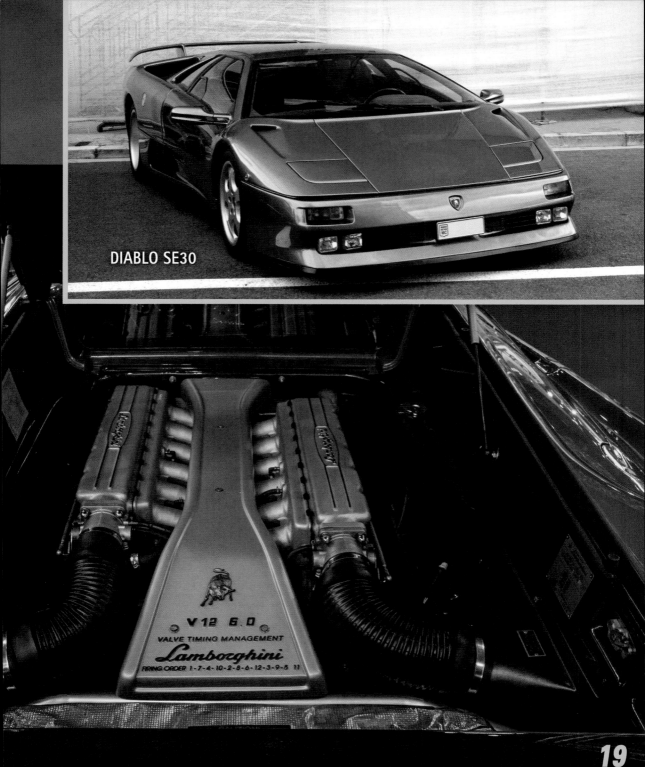

DIABLO SE30

V 12 6.0
VALVE TIMING MANAGEMENT
Lamborghini
FIRING ORDER 1-7-4-10-2-8-6-12-3-9-5-11

THE MURCIÉLAGO
2001–2010

The Murciélago was made to replace the Diablo. It was one of Lamborghini's most popular models. Many customers had to reserve their car in advance! *Murciélago* means "bat" in Spanish. The car, like many other Lamborghinis, was named after a famous fighting bull from the 19th century. The Murciélago was made from 2001 until 2010, and 4,099 cars were sold. The first Murciélago model was called simply the Lamborghini Murciélago. Later models had different names so people could tell them apart.

The 2001 Murciélago model could reach 60 miles (96.6 km) per hour in 3.6 seconds. It could get to 116 miles (186.7 km) per hour in 11.6 seconds. This Murciélago had a top speed of 205 miles (330 km) per hour. It had a V-12 engine that produced 580 horsepower.

THE LAST MURCIÉLAGO MODEL WAS INTRODUCED IN 2009. IT WAS CALLED THE MURCIÉLAGO LP670-4 SUPERVELOCE. IT COULD GO FROM 0 TO 62 MILES (0 TO 100 KM) IN 3.2 SECONDS AND HAD A TOP SPEED OF 212 MILES (341.2 KM) PER HOUR.

LP670-4 SUPERVELOCE

THE GALLARDO
2003–2013

The Gallardo made its debut at the 2003 Geneva Motor Show. It had a V-10 engine that produced 500 horsepower. The Gallardo was named after a famous breed of fighting bull rather than a specific bull's name. It was created to be an everyday sports car. The Gallardo was shorter than other Lamborghinis but still performed like the other cars. During the Gallardo's production, it was Lamborghini's best-selling car. More than 14,000 Gallardos were made.

The LP570-4 Superleggera, a type of Gallardo, was introduced in 2010. *Superleggera* means "super light" in Italian. The Superleggera had a top speed of 202 miles (325.1 km) per hour. It could go from 0 to 60 miles (0 to 96.6 km) per hour in 3.4 seconds and could get up to 124 miles (200 km) per hour in only 10.2 seconds.

THE LAST GALLARDO PRODUCED WAS A LP570-4 SPYDER PERFORMANTE LIKE THE ONES PICTURED HERE. HOWEVER, THAT FINAL ONE WAS PAINTED *ROSSO MARS* ("MARS RED" IN ITALIAN) AND SOLD TO A PRIVATE COLLECTOR.

THE AVENTADOR
2011–PRESENT

The Aventador was made to replace the Murciélago. It was launched on February 28, 2011, at the Geneva Motor Show. It's named after a famous fighting bull that earned an award for its courage during a bullfight in 1993. The car looks very similar to the limited-edition Murciélago-based Reventón.

THE AVENTADOR IS SO LOW TO THE GROUND THAT IT HAS A LIFTING SYSTEM THAT BRINGS THE CAR'S FRONT END UP 1.6 INCHES (4 CM) SO DRIVERS CAN GET OVER BUMPS SAFELY.

The Aventador LP700-4 Coupe has a powerful, hand-built, 6.5-liter V-12 engine that accelerates, or goes faster, quickly, reacts at lightning speed, and roars like no other Lamborghini before it. It produces 691 horsepower. The Aventador LP700-4 Coupe can go from 0 to 62 miles (0 to 100 km) per hour in just 2.9 seconds and has a top speed of 217 miles (349.2 km) per hour. It has all-wheel drive.

CURRENT
LAMBORGHINIS

In 2018, Lamborghini produced three different models of super sports cars: the Urus, the Huracán, and the Aventador. The Urus is a four-door, five-seat super sport utility vehicle. Its V-8 engine produces 650 horsepower. The Urus has a maximum speed of 189.5 miles (305 km) per hour and can go from 0 to 62 miles (0 to 100 km) per hour in just 3.6 seconds.

The Huracán is a two-seater that comes in six versions. The Huracán Performante, the fastest Huracán model, has a V-10 engine that produces 640 horsepower. It has a top speed of about 202 miles (325 km) per hour and can go from 0 to 62 miles (0 to 100 km) per hour in just 2.9 seconds.

THE URUS IS THE FIRST LAMBORGHINI SINCE 1988 TO HAVE A V-8 ENGINE. THE AVERAGE PRICE OF AN URUS, WITH UPGRADES FROM THE BASE MODEL, IS AROUND $225,000. IT'S ONE OF THE MOST EXPENSIVE SUVS ON THE MARKET.

LIMITED EDITIONS

As of 2018, Lamborghini produced three limited-edition cars called one-offs. The Centenario Roadster and Centenario have V-12 engines that produce 770 horsepower. They have a maximum speed of more than 217 miles (350 km) per hour and can go from 0 to 62 miles (0 to 100 km) per hour in just 2.9 seconds. The Veneno Roadster has a V-12 engine that produces 750 horsepower. It has a maximum speed of 221 miles (355.7 km) per hour and can also go from 0 to 62 miles (0 to 100 km) per hour in 2.9 seconds.

VENENO ROADSTER

THE FUTURE OF LAMBORGHINIS

Lamborghini has always worked to improve its cars. It continues to make its cars faster, more powerful, and more eye-catching. Today, Lamborghini is working on something big. The Terzo Millennio, which means "third millennium" in Italian, is a self-healing electric supercar. The Terzo Millennio debuted as a **concept** car at the EmTech conference in Cambridge, Massachusetts, on November 6, 2017. Lamborghini partnered with the Massachusetts Institute of Technology to create this car.

The Terzo Millennio has the signature Lamborghini wedge shape, but it also has a windshield that reaches far down the front end. It's able to tell when it's been harmed and the body will be able to heal small cracks. Lamborghini plans to create in-wheel electric motors so the car won't need one big engine. The Terzo Millennio is a Lamborghini of the future.

THE TERZO MILLENNIO RUNS ON ELECTRICITY INSTEAD OF GASOLINE. LAMBORGHINI WANTS TO CREATE A TYPE OF BATTERY CALLED A SUPERCAPACITOR TO STORE THE CAR'S ENERGY.

TIMELINE

April 28, 1916 ❯ Ferruccio Lamborghini is born in Cento, Italy.

May 1963 ❯ Ferruccio Lamborghini founds Automobili Ferruccio Lamborghini in Sant'Agata Bolognese, Italy.

November 1963 ❯ The Lamborghini 350 GTV prototype debuts at the Turin Auto Show.

1964 ❯ The 350 GT is launched.

1971 ❯ Ferruccio Lamborghini retires. The Countach prototype LP500 debuts at the Geneva Car Show.

1974 ❯ The Countach is launched.

1987 ❯ French Formula One team Larrousse asks designer Mauro Forghieri to create a new engine for its cars.

1990 ❯ The Diablo is launched.

February 20, 1993 ❯ Ferruccio Lamborghini dies in Perugia, Italy.

2001 ❯ The Murciélago is launched.

2003 ❯ The Gallardo is launched.

2011 ❯ The Aventador is launched.

November 6, 2017 ❯ The Terzo Millennio concept is on display at the EmTech conference.

2018 ❯ Lamborghini sells three models: the Huracán, the Aventador, and the Urus.

||| GLOSSARY |||

astrological: Having to do with astrology, or the study of how the positions of the stars and movements of the planets have a supposed effect on events and people.

concept: Created to show an idea.

cylinder: A tube-shaped part of an engine where power is created.

design: The way something has been made. Also, to create the plan for something.

edition: One of the forms in which something is presented.

endurance: The quality of continuing for a long time.

futuristic: Being or looking like the style or type of something that people think things might look like in years to come.

innovation: A new way of doing things.

mechanic: A person who makes or repairs machines.

prance: To spring from the back legs or move by doing so.

prototype: A first or early example that is used as a model for what comes later.

signature: Something, such as a quality or feature, that is closely associated with someone or something.

symbol: Something that stands for something else.

version: A form of something that is different from the ones that came before it.

III INDEX III

III WEBSITES III

Due to the changing nature of Internet links, PowerKids Press has developed an online list of websites related to the subject of this book. This site is updated regularly. Please use this link to access the list: www.powerkidslinks.com/hood/lambos